Character by Design

Jeanne Shafer

Which shall it be:
Character by *Design* or
Character by *Default?*

TEACH Services, Inc.
PUBLISHING
www.TEACHServices.com • (800) 367-1844

World rights reserved. This book or any portion thereof may not be copied or reproduced in any form or manner whatever, except as provided by law, without the written permission of the publisher, except by a reviewer who may quote brief passages in a review.

The author assumes full responsibility for the accuracy of all facts and quotations as cited in this book. The opinions expressed in this book are the author's personal views and interpretations, and do not necessarily reflect those of the publisher.

This book is provided with the understanding that the publisher is not engaged in giving spiritual, legal, medical, or other professional advice. If authoritative advice is needed, the reader should seek the counsel of a competent professional.

Copyright © 2019 Jeanne Shafer
Copyright © 2019 TEACH Services, Inc.
ISBN-13: 978-1-4796-1058-7 (Paperback)
ISBN-13: 978-1-4796-1059-4 (ePub)
Library of Congress Control Number: 2019908097

All Bible references are taken from the Authorized (King James) Version (AKJV) unless otherwise stated. Reproduced by permission of Cambridge University Press, the Crown's patentee in the UK.

Bible references marked (NIV) are taken from the Holy Bible, New International Version®, NIV® Copyright ©1973, 1978, 1984, 2011 by Biblica, Inc.® Used by permission. All rights reserved worldwide.

www.TEACHServices.com • (800) 367-1844

In Review

"In these pages I discovered God's own design for the family in the Christian home. In a simple and practical way, the author has brought to life the government of the family and its relationship to the heavenly Father and His church. The emphasis is on the application of these principles in the everyday life of the family, and how, with the Holy Spirit's influence, the desired character may be developed from the very start of life. The author also reinforces the fact that Love is the fulfillment of the law in the home and family, as it is in heaven. As a mother and grandmother, as well as Mental Health Counselor, I highly recommend this beautifully written book that reveals the precepts of true education, bringing lasting benefits to any family."

—Judith Powers, Mental Health Counselor, Keno, Oregon

"When I was given the opportunity to read ***Character by Design,*** I knew that this is and will be an invaluable resource and great blessing to any parent, educator and spiritual leader, even a child or student desiring to understand and implement God's Character Building Plan for a life of fulfillment and service!"

—William G.H. Paùl,
Wellness Educator, Husband and Father, Chiliquin, Oregon

"My mother's parents took a course called 'Childhood Education' at Berrien Springs, Michigan in the summer of 1904. This course was taught in the apple orchard on the ground that was broken for Emmanuel Missionary College that very year. The teacher of that course was Ellen G. White. My mother at eight years of age came to know Sister White personally when she would come to Madison College and give worship talks. After reading your booklet, ***Character by Design,*** it reminded me of all that I had heard about the course that my grandparents had taken from Sister White. Consequently, I have a great appreciation for your book, for it will be a great blessing to those who search its pages. The world is in great need of this very help while Christian parents endeavor to raise the children that God has lent them to raise for His kingdom. He will greatly reward you for working in harmony with Him to put this instructional book into circulation. All God's grace and blessings to you, then through you."

—Darrel and Dorothy Manning, Retired, Milburn, Oklahoma

Table of Contents

Dedication 7
Foreword 9
"Feed My Lambs" 13
Chapter 1: Of Babes and Sucklings 17
Chapter 2: The Righteousness That Maketh a
    Child Righteous 23
Chapter 3: Lullaby … and Good Night 29
Chapter 4: "Train Up a Child in the Way He Should Go …" 39
Chapter 5: Of Little Acorns and Mighty Oaks 49
Then, What About Punishment? 59
"Practical Applications" 1, 2, 3, 4 61
Summary 71

Dedicated to

Every Dear Christian Family

Whose feet are set on the Bright Path

To their Father's House.

May His TRUTH guide you

And His LOVE sustain you

All the way home.

—The Author

CHARACTER BY DESIGN:

"Jesus is drawing the children, and He bids us, 'suffer them to come,' as if He would say, 'They will come if you do not hinder them'" (White, *The Desire of Ages,* p. 517.2).

Foreword

"These letters are addressed to parents, yet they require a much broader interest involving friends, extended family - the fellowship of faith; because the responsibility for the education of our children, while appointed primarily to the parents, rests also upon this extended family, and requires that their influence upon these little ones be supportive of the parents, under God, in their challenging task."

We often wish for a voice of experience to tell us just how to meet all the everyday situations that are the fabric of life in every family with children, sensing that the outcome of some small crisis has larger consequences down the road, and that the way it is handled is of critical importance. In our search for help we may find many resources—traditional and contemporary, scientific as well as religious. But to find practical applications, we soon discover that it is essential to uncover the supporting principles, because too often standard formulas do not fit the divine pattern.

These messages to our beloved young parents are intended to set forth principles that must be understood and acted on understandingly if they are to succeed. Parents often look for standardized formulas that they think will enable them to be successful, rather than taking the time or making the commitment to uncover *underlying principles.* Consequently, God is often hindered from giving them what they most desire. Yet it is these divine principles that would allow them as parents the freedom, under the Holy Spirit's guidance, to proceed promptly, effectively, and with perfect confidence, in every unique situation.

Thankfully, the answers we need are all close at hand, and they are perfectly revealed in the everlasting gospel. The truth for God's people now is thrilling in its distinctive promise of restoration—and it is particularly relevant to the home. And as we bring the great principles of the law of love into our service as parents and educators, we are promised heavenly support and success. This is what we want to share with you—the absolute integrity of these enduring elements that underly every command of God. We can testify to their practicality. And the promise of victory is sure.

As the community of faith learns to work harmoniously on this basis, then the labors of parents and guardians will be effective. The victories gained in the school of the home will not be negated by unthinking or ignorant social influences from the larger communion. And as we study the methods of the gospel for the sake of the children, we will be rewarded by a fresh understanding ourselves, for *"whosoever shall not receive the kingdom of God as a little child, he shall not enter therein"* (Mark 10:15).

—JS

The Order of the Gospel in the Family
and in the Church
OR
The Plan of True Education For
"THE LITTLE FLOCK"

"Feed My Lambs"

The Charge:

"And ye shall know that I have sent this commandment unto you, that my covenant ... was with him of life and peace; and I gave them to him for the fear wherewith he feared me, and was afraid before my name. The law of truth was in his mouth, and iniquity was not found in his lips: he walked with me in peace and equity, and did turn many away from iniquity. For the priest's lips should keep knowledge, and they should seek the law at his mouth: for he is the messenger of the Lord of hosts" (Malachi 2:4–7).

Appointments:

FATHER—Appointed by Christ as an administrator, the father is not only the provider; he is the governor of the family, prudently overseeing the educational structure as it was divinely appointed. Overall, upholding the morale of the family by demonstrating divine love.

MOTHER—The Consort: Appointed by Christ to preserve a Spirit-filled refuge where order and peace reign; managing the educational structure as a faithful mistress of all that is virtuous. As queen of the home, guiding the earliest training and habits of the children in their innocence: feeding, clothing, and cultivating emotional temperaments that uphold the morale of the family. Overall, cherishing all the attributes that divine love has prepared the mother to demonstrate.

ELDERS—Experienced guides: To preserve the law in the family and to escort parents in the fulfillment of the divine injunction: "Remember the days of old, consider the years of many generations: *ask thy father, and he will shew thee; thy elders, and they will tell thee*" (Deuteronomy 32:7, emphasis added).

"And what nation is there so great, that hath statutes and judgments so righteous as all this law, which I set before you this day? Only take heed to thyself, and keep thy soul diligently, lest thou forget the things which thine eyes have seen, and lest they depart from thy heart all the days of thy life: *but teach them thy sons, and thy son's sons* ... Gather me the people together, and I will make them hear my words, that they may learn to fear me all the days that they shall live upon the earth, and that they may teach them to their children" (Deuteronomy 4:8–10, emphasis added).

With Letters to Young Parents

"...Yea; have ye never read, Out of the mouth of babes and sucklings thou hast perfected praise?" (Matthew 21:16).

CHAPTER 1:
Of Babes and Sucklings

On an unforgettable spring day, long ago, we notice a procession forming on the path from the Mount of Olives into Jerusalem. A man of noble bearing is being prepared to ride an unbroken donkey, with his dam, into the city. Lazarus, just a few days before restored to life by the man who mounts the quiet beast, takes the reins and leads the animal forward. A crowd is gathering, and as they see what is happening, a spirit of joy and celebration takes hold. The people are placing their outer garments on the colt and gathering the branches of the palm trees lining the road, strewing them in the path of the procession. The little children catch the spirit, and in their enthusiasm are skipping and shouting, waving the palm branches, and singing the prophetic words exalting their dear Friend, "Hosanna to the Son of David: Blessed is he that cometh in the name of the Lord; Hosanna in the highest" (Matthew 21:9).

The following morning *it is the children again* who lead out in the joyous demonstrations, as Jesus engages in a glorious day of restoration, comfort, and teaching for that throng of suffering ones, who come seeking Christ's healing power. The Temple courts have been sternly emptied of the noise and confusion of the unholy trafficking that had desecrated the hallowed precincts, and in their place are heard shouts of praise and thanksgiving from those who are being healed, blending with the carefree abandon of the children's delight as they catch the spirit of the occasion. Their sunny songs of praise, their glowing enthusiasm, and waving palm branches magnify the scene, as they praise their dearest Friend and gentle Healer.

In their place are heard shouts of praise and thanksgiving from those who are being healed, blending with the carefree abandon of the children's delight as they catch the spirit of the occasion.

Soon, upon hearing the commotion, the guilty priests and rulers of the Temple cautiously find their way back to this amazing scene. Alarmed for their own safety and with anxious feelings, yet hoping still to ensnare Jesus in some way by His answers, they boldly accost Jesus and demand, "Do you hear what these children are saying?"

And the calm, confident reply of Jesus, "Yea; have ye never read, *Out of the mouth of babes and sucklings thou hast perfected praise?*" (Matthew 21:16, emphasis added).

The significance of this response gives us pause—doesn't it? —as we think in terms of the Holy Spirit's influence on the newborn nursling, as well as the babe still in the womb. Consider Jacob, who prophetically clung to his brother Esau's heel at birth; Samson, whose parents were so carefully instructed as to his prenatal care; Jeremiah, that "weeping prophet" for Israel in its captivity, sanctified and ordained to his prophetic office *before he was born*, called in his youth to be a mouthpiece for God in that critical time; John the Baptist, who leaped for joy in the womb of Elisabeth, as Mary, newly pregnant with Jesus, greeted her cousin; and above all, *Christ Himself, conceived and born of the Holy Ghost*—all this sacred history has been preserved for our learning, with important lessons for those in our time, who look for practical, spiritual guidelines in how to prepare their little ones to fulfill their place in God's plan.

When the mother has brought forth her child and provides for its basic needs—food and warmth and love—she has but just begun her special role of motherhood. We see that *the spiritual nature is already in place at birth*, awaiting the cooperation of the new parents to bring it to its maturity, with the guidance of the Holy Ghost all along the way. To the godly mother, in her special appointed way, is given the happy task of working together with the Holy Spirit toward forming a strong foundation for the developing spiritual nature of the child, thus pre-empting the design of Satan and "giving [him] no chance to control the minds and dispositions of these little ones" and so bringing forth a lovely, well-balanced character to the glory of the Creator (White, *Child Guidance*, p. 230.3).

CHAPTER 1: Of Babes and Sucklings

How does this process take place, and how soon may we begin? What may be expected of a young baby without vocabulary, without knowledge, without experience? How shall we prepare for its first lessons? To start with, the wonderful bond that is developing so beautifully between mother and child needs to be preserved and strengthened in this process. Then we will discover as we go, that the *formation of positive habits* will be a primary tool in the hands of the mother as she proceeds. How carefully the patterns of these habits must be chosen, with forethought and understanding, in order that they may be used as an unchanging foundation for all future development.

This new little intelligence is like a fresh, white page, ready to be written on with true, unvarying principles. In the process there will be steady development of concepts and vocabulary, as the dawning of intellect awakens naturally, little by little, to the impressions that each day brings. Each experience, each impression, is like a building block, to be fixed carefully in place, one at a time, strengthening the structure to support continuing development.

Must the mother tax her mind to develop a *curriculum* to follow for this education? Rather, it will soon become apparent that nature itself has prepared many favorable moments for the parent who is open to the guidance of the Spirit, and understands how to make use of these natural openings. And these lessons may be learned without diminishing the precious bond between mother and child. In fact, rightly met, each successful experience enriches this bond significantly. And here is where Mother needs perfect freedom to engage in these critical exercises. The home nest[1], rather than busy gatherings, lends itself best to those valuable, spontaneous, and divinely ordained incidents where lifelong victories may be secured. **They are best met in the moment and in the Spirit, for they may never be repeated.**

To illustrate, let's take a hypothetical situation that many mothers can relate to, as an example of a favorable moment for a first lesson in *self-government*. In principle, each of these "favorable moments" is an opportunity to engage in developing a baby character capable of making personal decisions—one small step at a time—even at a very tender age. These small victories enhance and confirm an ever-increasing bond with their heavenly Father, through the Holy Spirit.

Let us suppose then that the early weeks and months have been used to advantage in forming a routine to encourage good patterns of eating, sleeping, and happy wakefulness and interaction with Mother and family.

---

1   See "The Environmental Atmosphere" in chapter three.

Early little issues that may have come up with sleep and eating patterns are being resolved with careful management, and all is going well. Now Baby has just erupted his first tooth, and Mother has provided suitable teething toys to relieve those tender little gums. At this moment he is nursing well and is happy in Mother's arms. Suddenly the little one bites down on the breast—hard! And this natural response to that unfamiliar little tooth in his mouth simply must be tried, it seems. But, oh, ouch! What shall be done? Is this just a normal reaction that must be endured by Mother, or should she try to divert his attention until she feels he is old enough to understand, and hope that will do for the present? Or should she play a little game that changes the focus? But what would that accomplish? It would only delay the action to be tried again later, after an innocent trial has gained approval through acceptance—doing "whatever feels good" is OK as long as nobody complains. These tendencies, which become more firmly entrenched with repetition, will fast gain in strength, only to ripen into undesirable behaviors—where the gentler corrections must give way to ever stronger incentives—and at last grow into firm habits hard to "break." Furthermore, this delay means that a valuable advantage in self-government has been lost.

Is it possible that a message can be sent right here that will teach in a simple but memorable, way the inappropriateness of this action? Is baby really ready to receive his first understanding of Mother's authority in obedience and submission to her position? No force or punishment shall be used, but the lesson will be enduringly impressed upon the infant mind. In the process the child's will must not be crushed, but rather strengthened and supported through a positive experience.

Now let's continue this little tableau: Upon the first trial, Mother says with a strong tone of voice she has never before used, **"Don't bite!"** At this unexpected turn of events, baby looks up, startled. Immediately the action is interrupted. He seems to think, "What does this mean? Something new is going on here...." Baby considers this for a moment, but after a little hesitation he gets back to business. Pretty soon he innocently bites once more. And now he hears that sound again, *"NO!"* This time it registers. Mother is not to be trifled with. This calm and sensitive mother, herself resigned to the Holy Spirit, confidently follows up her command with attention-getting action (perhaps a light flick of the finger on the little cheek?). Now his unapproved action has been stopped, and he has been awakened to a new experience in *loving discipleship.* It has taken place without force, or punishment, with only the gentlest *correction* necessary to gain attention, giving this young *Suckling* the opportunity to take personal responsibility for his own actions.

But that gentle correction has seemed to interrupt the beautiful and comforting relationship with Mother, and a trembling chin and tearful eyes touch her sympathy. And notice, she does not hesitate to console the small offender, just as the Good Shepherd comforts the wayward lamb. Then there is submission and resignation, and the blessed connection is restored. Victory for all! As he responds to this light correction, he experiences something of what it means to respond to Mother's will. The precious bond with Mother remains intact, while he is gradually being set free to be personally responsible for his behavior.

Love triumphs once again. The way is prepared for ongoing instruction and victories as maturity develops. With consistency, and a wise and loving tutor, Baby grows in grace. He learns what to expect, and how to avoid disturbing a cherished relationship, *by respecting the law;* yes, and even catches something of the peace and satisfaction of self-denial.

And so we observe, in this simple illustration, how the Holy Spirit and the mother may work together, naturally and effectively, in awakening the first God-fearing responses of a little one, as life unlocks its spiritual treasures bit-by-bit. And while each mother may not exactly duplicate this experience, she may easily, *once the principle is grasped,* make application to each unique circumstance. Beginning in the sacred relationships of childhood, personal accountability is gradually developed, *to be perfected in the fear of the Lord* throughout life. And interestingly, no artificial test needs to be contrived. Nature has provided the opportunity, and the Holy Spirit has acted—*on the mother first,* as she has surrendered to His influence, and *then on the child,* to bring about perfect satisfaction for the law.

> *With consistency, and a wise and loving tutor, Baby grows in grace. He learns what to expect, and how to avoid disturbing a cherished relationship, by respecting the law; yes, and even catches something of the peace and satisfaction of self-denial.*

Yours for Perfecting Praise in Babes and Sucklings …

"Day by day parents should learn
in the school of Christ lessons from
One that loves them. Then the story of God's
everlasting love will be repeated in the home school
to the tender flock. Thus, before reason is
fully developed, children may catch a right
spirit from their parents"
(White, Child Guidance, pp. 26.5).

CHAPTER 2:
The Righteousness That Maketh A Child Righteous

Dear Young Parents of the Lord's Household,

Early in 1853, two pioneer preachers were traveling in Wisconsin looking for a group of believers. After visits with other isolated believers, they came to Koshkonong, where there was a company of twenty, the largest number of any in one place in the state. They had the name of the most prominent one among them, and as they neared the settlement, inquired for him. Finally, they saw a man in a cornfield near the road of whom they hoped to ask directions. Elder Cornell said to Elder Loughborough, "I'm going to ask that man the question asked in the Apocrypha of the Old Testament." First, he inquired for the home of Milton Southwick, whom they were seeking. The man said, "He lives in the second house from here." Elder Cornell then asked his question: "Has 'righteousness that maketh a man righteous' been through this land?" An interesting question by Elder Cornell! And the man rightly took it as referring to the Law of God. The man, it happened, was Elder Phelps, leader of their company. "Yes!" he replied. "There are a few of us here who are trying to keep all of the commandments of God. Are you not the brethren from the East of whom we read in the *Review* who are coming to Wisconsin?"[2]

---

2   Story taken from *Miracles in My Life* by J.N. Loughborough, p. 34.

These people were trying to keep the commandments, and now they were waiting for God's messengers to perfect their understanding.

The prophet Joel, in chapter 2:23 [margin], refers to this righteousness in the promise of the latter rain. Believers have waited a long time for this scripture to be fulfilled, and now here we are, living in the very time of the latter rain, eagerly expecting the imminent fulfillment of these rich and precious promises. You may be wondering what practical application we may find in this impressive prophecy. Do we have a part to act in its fulfillment? And what will it mean in our personal experience, in the family, and in the community of faith?

There's an important clue found in Malachi 4:5, 6. Here we find the "Elijah message," so closely connected with the promise of the latter rain: "Behold, I will send you Elijah the prophet before the coming of the great and dreadful day of the LORD: And He shall turn the heart of the fathers to the children, and the heart of the children to their fathers, lest I come and smite the earth with a curse." This message is intended to prepare God's remnant for the coming of Jesus, and the first thing it does is to turn the hearts of the fathers to the children. So we see that the "restoration" begins in the family! The testimony of the Lord confirms this. The "great reformatory movement must begin in presenting to fathers and mothers and children the principles of the law of God" (White, *Testimonies for the Church*, vol. 6, p. 119). "...The teaching of righteousness that maketh a man righteous."[3]

Now when the heart of the father is turned to the children, his first work is to establish order—gospel order—in his home. He will accept and cherish his duty as the spiritual leader and priest of his family.

> *Now when the heart of the father is turned to the children, his first work is to establish order—gospel order—in his home. He will accept and cherish his duty as the spiritual leader and priest of his family.*

Appreciating the natural capacities of the mother in the early education of their little ones, he will recognize her responsibilities according to the divine appointment. He knows that it is her commission to lay the groundwork in "the teaching of righteousness

---

3   Joel 2:23 marginal reference by Elder Loughborough, *Miracles in My Life*, p. 34.

CHAPTER 2: The Righteousness That Maketh A Child Righteous

that maketh (shall we say a child?) righteous." She is the first teacher of her newborn. To her belongs in a special sense the care and training of the baby from its birth. Hers is the accountability for the beginnings of his education, for teaching him *the spirit of the law* in every tender ministration. She must subdue its will, by capturing her baby with love—in order that she may set him free. She must establish habits of purity, of attentiveness, order, and loving obedience. It is, after all, habit that defines character. It is given to the mother to lead her child into those fine habits that are its building blocks; and she is freely supported by the wise and well-informed father. When these building blocks are laid on the foundation of pure love, it fulfills the divine law, and the structure indeed is fit for the heavenly kingdom.

As the child grows out of babyhood, well-grounded physically and morally, the father picks up his responsibilities in a new way, in his strength and authority augmenting the mother's efforts in giving suitable nutriment to the developing spiritual nature, shaping the growing child's personality, helping him to integrate into the larger communion, the family of God, and preparing him for his life work on earth and for the eternal life hereafter. As the family priest, his *"lips should keep knowledge, and they should seek the law at his mouth: for he is the messenger of the L*ORD *of hosts"* (Malachi 2:7). This cooperative endeavor is the wonderful pattern that is given to us, the setting in which takes place "the teaching of righteousness that maketh a (child) righteous."

In order to become teachers of righteousness, parents and guardians must *be* what they wish their *children to become.* Jesus stated an eternal principle when He said, *"The Son can do nothing of himself, but what he seeth the Father do: for what things soever he doeth, these also the Son doeth likewise. For the Father loveth the Son, and sheweth him all things that himself doeth ..."* (John 5:19, 20).

If parents themselves are subject to the law, if they have that willing obedience (the obedience that is the result of the power of the will, in captivity to love), they will then be able to apply the law with confidence. Their own experience as pupils of the Holy Spirit will prepare them to educate the will of their children, and to "train their [children] to feel that the power lies in themselves to become men and women of honor and usefulness" (White, *Fundamentals of Christian Education*, p. 58).

How does the power lie within themselves? Philippians 2:12, 13 directs us to "work out your own salvation with fear and trembling. For it is God which worketh in you both to will and to do of his good pleasure." Since parents are to be as God to their children in their early years, do they not work in their children to will and to do of *their* good pleasure? Listen to this, from the *Desire of Ages*, page 669:

"All true obedience comes from the heart. It was heart work with Christ. And if we consent, He will so identify Himself with our thoughts and aims, so blend our hearts and minds into conformity to His will, that when obeying Him we shall be but carrying out our own impulses. The will, refined and sanctified, will find its highest delight in doing His service. When we know God as it is our privilege to know Him, our life will be a life of continual obedience."

And so with the little children. When their will has been captured by love, it becomes empowered to do right. When obeying they "will be but carrying out their own impulses."

Now, in order not to enforce obedience upon us, God uses only those methods that honor individual choice. True home education also limits itself, in order to respect the individuality of even little children. The principles of love and authority are limited only by the respect due to their individuality, to appreciate the power of choice. In limiting ourselves for the children's sake, as God limits Himself for our sakes, we won't be afraid to hold in check our own power and control; we won't hesitate to relinquish our methods of coercion, competition, or permissiveness; we won't be afraid to "let go" for fear it might not work. We will know by experience that the divine principles will work. The law of education is inseparable from moral and natural law, the laws of liberty, faith, and love. It is eternal. As we move into the divine order, we will discover the practicality of these concepts. God has given us abundant direction in His Word, if we know how to look for it and recognize it. And He has given us the key to all knowledge. David expresses it like this:

"Open thou mine eyes, that I may behold wondrous things out of thy law. ... O how love I thy law! it is my meditation all the day. Thou through thy commandments hast made me wiser than mine enemies ... I have more understanding than all my teachers: for thy testimonies are my meditation. I understand more than the ancients, because I keep thy precepts. ... Through thy precepts I get understanding ..." (Psalm 119:18, 97–100, 104).

If we as parents are "taught by God" (NIV), we will have at our fingertips—virtually springing from our hearts—unerring methods and applications. If the gospel is not practical to us, we may employ the most ancient and venerable educational systems, or the most contemporary scientific methods, but our children's minds and souls will never be liberated to go beyond the narrow confines of what the world calls "higher education."

CHAPTER 2: The Righteousness That Maketh A Child Righteous

We have heard many of these things for years, but now it is time for us to bring them into our hearts and homes. This is the time of "the restoration of all things" and the "great reformatory movement must begin in presenting to fathers and mothers and children the principles of the law of God" — "the teaching of righteousness that maketh (a family, a child, a communion) righteous." And may we not rightly expect divine power to bring about this long-awaited reformation?

Yours in joyful anticipation ...

"As the mother teaches her children to obey her because they love her, she is teaching them the first lessons in the Christian life. The mother's love represents to the child the love of Christ, and the little ones who trust and obey their mother are learning to trust and obey the Saviour" (White, *The Desire of Ages*, p. 515.4).

CHAPTER 3:
Lullaby ... and Good Night ...

Dear Young Parents of the Lord's Household,
What's in a lullaby? What is it about the charming cradlesongs that are such an endearing part of every culture around the world? Indeed, many lullabies have crossed cultural barriers to become classics that have lulled babies to sleep for generations. This beguiling, universal art has always held a special place in our hearts. And might it not, in its purest, truest form, serve as a valuable element in our plan of "Character by Design"?

Most of us have heard these familiar maxims: "From babyhood the character of the child is to be molded and fashioned in accordance with the divine plan." (White, *Child Guidance*, p. 193.2.) "The work of the mother must commence at an early age, giving Satan no chance to control the minds and dispositions of their little ones." (White, *Child Guidance*, p. 230.3)"One of the first lessons a child needs to learn is the lesson of obedience. Before he is old enough to reason, he may be taught to obey."(White, *Child Guidance*, p. 82.4.) And again, "Parents, you should commence your first lesson of discipline when your children are babes in your arms. Teach them to yield their will to yours. This can be done by bearing an even hand and manifesting firmness." (White, *Child Guidance*, p. 230.4.)

Sometimes these beautiful ideals seem almost intimidating, the standard is so high. But you are motivated, because the little one in your arms may already be stiffening his little back and screaming in obvious anger, and your earnest question is, *"How can I carry out these principles? Surely a small baby can't be disciplined?! He can't reason yet, or even understand what I say—and punishment is out of the question." "Show me how,"* is your plea. *"Make it practical!"*

You need a customized approach. And we find it—yes, in the gospel. It's remarkable how the principles of the gospel and the teachings and example of Jesus provide the direction and support we need. It's true, we want to pattern acceptable behavior, but let's lead our children to Jesus, where they learn to obey out of love for Him rather than from fear of punishment.

And we can't begin too soon! Love is the foundation of all true education, and it isn't hard to love our babies! *When we as parents dwell in Christ,* we meet their needs in the true, principled way that reflects His love to them so engagingly. As they learn to submit to our will, the law of love ensures that they will acquire the habit of obedience—first to the mother and the father, then to God.

So let's recap some of the premises of the gospel, and see how they work in our favor. Sleep time is the perfect setting for our demonstration, since "Go to sleep" is probably Mother's first command. Because nature cooperates by inducing sleep, there is already a natural readiness, a primary principle of true education, that will work to our advantage. We'll soon see how lullabies may serve to help a mother meet these objectives.

> *Love is the foundation of all true education, and it isn't hard to love our babies!*

First, though, to respect the individuality of our children we will limit ourselves to three divine educational principles. And these principles are valid not only for the older child, but for the babe in arms as well. Through them communication is established, even before language and reasoning skills are learned. They will serve us well in laying the right foundation:

1. THE ENVIRONMENTAL ATMOSPHERE.
2. THE DISCIPLINE OF HABIT.
3. THE INTRODUCTION OF LIVING IDEAS.

As we limit ourselves to these guidelines, we find the principles of the gospel exemplified perfectly, and they will help us to nurture the God-given individuality of our children.

We often hear about "controlling our children," but if parents supply an environment under the control of the Holy Spirit, the children tend to reflect this Spirit and submit to His control. What we want is not to force our will upon the child, which will only crush his own will, but to *train his will*—to energize it. We want to place the law before our children in its beauty, and then set them free to obey. Mother does not conquer the child's temper—he fights his own battle with self even at a very early age and finds rest and satisfaction in the victory. He discovers the first principle of a sanctified will—to distinguish between "I want" and "I will." It is as we recognize *his God-given right to choose* that he finds freedom to obey, that his will becomes energized, and he discovers the joy and satisfaction of understanding and obeying his mother's commands.

The newborn's world is in sharp contrast to the safe, warm, secure environment in which he has developed throughout gestation. Yet there is still something familiar and comforting that gives him a sense of continuity and security. His mother is still the central focus—though no longer all—and the two are still interdependent, emotionally as well as physically. But as he was set free of the womb at birth, so the mother's goal now is gradually to set her little one's personality free during these years of his increasing accountability (which is really working for his conversion), and in this liberating process the child is learning to take increasing responsibility for his own actions. He is learning that he is an individual in his own right, God's own child, and accountable to Him, first of all.

Don't worry that you will lose your baby's love as he gains this liberty. On the contrary, you'll find that your relationship will continually mature and deepen. Mutual appreciation and respect will increase throughout childhood, adolescence, and adulthood, because you respect your child's individuality—and he sees in you the helper of his joy. He loves you for helping him gain self-reliance and confidence, and for teaching him to find delight in service and submission to proper authority. He learns that Mother and Father can always be trusted; they never take advantage of his innocence and are reliable and consistent. They do not try to dominate him, but carefully guide him into self-control, empowered by the Holy Spirit.

Now let's see how our three educational tools may be used to develop primary patterns and to encourage positive responses. This is accomplished in the earliest weeks and months very simply. In the small baby's interaction with Mother he gains his first concept of authority carried out in principled love. For it is the mother's place to teach *the spirit of the law* in every tender ministration. How does she do this? Let's begin with preparation.

Even before baby arrives, "THE ENVIRONMENTAL ATMOSPHERE" is considered. The nursery will be furnished simply, free of gaudy artificials, ruffles, and fanciful figures. Clean, sweet, uncluttered, functional, warm, it radiates a natural beauty. It is planned for Baby's response, and for Mother's convenience, so she can be free to work without hindrance and distraction. Her role there is top priority—Baby comes first. For the time being, it's more important than doorbells, messaging, and ordinary calls for her attention. As Mother resigns her own spirit, giving her undivided attention to this vital undertaking, the heavenly Spirit graces this first little environment with calmness and peace.

Now she will enlist the "DISCIPLINE OF HABIT," beginning immediately to move toward the routine that will enhance the smooth functioning of the household. The formation of good habit is probably the most painless part of DISCIPLING. Mother knows this instinctively, it seems, and wisely studies the unique character of her baby and designs a feeding, rest, and activity routine that will maximize its own physical, mental, and moral development, using every natural advantage to promote her ends. And these are many ... *ritual*, for example—always doing the same thing, in the same way, at the same time, in the same place. A sample might be this little introductory routine (which always happens in the nursery environment until Baby's development indicates that it's time for expanded horizons):

1. Close door.
2. Feed, burp.
3. Change diaper in designated place.
4. Wrap snugly in blanket.
5. Hold in arms, kiss, talk lovingly, and place in cradle.

The little one is led steadily and naturally to comply with this enjoyable routine, and it is Mother's responsibility to make it a pleasant experience. After all, love, obedience, and joy are inseparable, and here is where baby first learns this principle. When it's time for a nap, Mother takes him into her arms and uses her most powerful ally, LOVE, to woo him to slumberland. Reconciled, and at peace herself, she becomes a channel through which the Holy Spirit communicates righteousness to her child, using the natural avenues to his mind that he understands:

1. **Touch**: Soft, tender, soothing; kisses, gentle hugs, caresses; snug swaddling for the first few weeks; soft, warm receiving blanket; sleep-inducing swaying, rocking motions.

2. **Taste**: Mother's own warm, sweet, satisfying milk.

3. **Sight**: Surroundings uncluttered, soft light, quiet colors, smile and pleasant look on Mother's face.

4. **Sound**: All quiet and peaceful, allowing the child to focus on Mother's tender voice, her soothing words, with beguiling melodies and rhythms as desired, to lull to sleep.

5. **Smell**: Pure surroundings; no offending odors—pleasant, natural scents.

A healthy newborn usually falls asleep as soon as he is fed. But sometimes after a short period of sleep he will wake up crying. Foresight and preparedness often help to ensure uninterrupted rest. Seasoned mothers tell us that "feeding full" leaves less room for air bubbles, and therefore helps to avoid one of the causes for "colic." Then, with a final "burp" before allowing baby to fall asleep, a last check to be sure his clothing is comfortable, and not too warm or too cool (especially keep the head covered with a light bonnet for the first few weeks to keep body temperature equalized; the baby's sleeping room can have open windows even in cool weather if the head is covered and protected from drafts). Be sure the diaper is clean and dry. If a change is needed, he may fuss through the changing process, but if this activity disturbs his initial sleepiness, a little rocking or patting usually suffices to settle him down again.

After the "newborn" stage you might partly darken the room and close the door to provide an atmosphere conducive to sleep, and as he gets older, it will accustom him to being alone in the room without fear. Just be sure you're always near to hear the first sign of wakefulness, so he won't have to get all worked up and frantic trying to get attention. It's reassuring to find Mother always there when he wakes up, ready to meet his needs promptly. Then he has no opportunity or reason to become fearful. When it's time to wake up, make this a happy reunion by your cheerful words and affectionate hugs.

Will all this attention spoil him? Won't he learn to expect instant gratification if he never has to wait? Actually, anticipating his needs in advance and being prepared to meet them as they arise creates security, and develops his ability to be patient. He knows that his wants are consistently cared for, and there's no need to be fretful. If you wait until he cries, he soon learns that crying is a very effective way to get what he wants. Taking care of his needs on time—before he gets all worked up—reinforces your routine. It prepares an environment that will save you much time and labor, as well as frustration. When it's feeding time, have everything ready in advance so he doesn't have to wait while you attend to things that should already have been prepared, and he'll soon learn that he doesn't need to scream for attention.

At first, you'll probably want to put him to sleep right after feeding, so preparation also means having the changing table well supplied with fresh diapers (and don't forget powder, lotion, cleansing cloths, and a place for soiled diapers). Then you'll avoid the stress of running around with a baby in one arm, while trying to gather together all your props with the other. Be sure, too, that the bedding is folded back out of the way in advance, and the sheets are sweet and clean, so that when he has finally dropped off to sleep you can lay him in the crib with a minimum of disturbance. You see how this eliminates most of his need to cry? He is developing a most valuable *habit of contentment*, and the spoiling we so much feared will never have a chance to develop. This also makes the most economical use of your own time and energy.

If the spirit of the environment is carefully controlled, the DISCIPLINE OF HABIT will soon be established, and before long you and your baby should be settled into a happy routine. He will soon be ready to be placed directly into his crib with minimal preliminaries.

> *If the spirit of the environment is carefully controlled, the DISCIPLINE OF HABIT will soon be established, and before long you and your baby should be settled into a happy routine.*

But maybe your baby is a few weeks older, and he is beginning to be more aware of his surroundings, and to resist sleep in order to enjoy these new sensations. Also, he may not require as much sleep as before. Being a wise mother, you will take into account this development and adjust the routine accordingly. Night feedings will soon be dropped, and naptimes adjusted in relationship to his new needs. But you will still be in control of the situation. How? Through THE ENVIRONMENTAL ATMOSPHERE and the DISCIPLINE OF HABIT.

And now, "THE INTRODUCTION OF LIVING IDEAS." The baby is already accustomed to falling asleep under controlled conditions. So, at the predetermined time—after you've made proper preparation—just take him in your arms and begin talking. He won't understand what you're saying at first, but he'll learn to pick up on your intentions very quickly if you are consistent. Tell him you love him, that he's the dearest baby in the world, and now it's time to "go to sleep." Even without the advantage of verbal understanding, you are *introducing living ideas* through spirit and action.

Let your voice be soft and pleasant—more soothing than exciting—and he will soon succumb. Allow this time of closeness to lead you into your child's mind, to help you understand his reactions and respond accordingly. Is he perhaps stiffening his back to look around the room? Bring him back gently to resting position and coax him to relax. Does he test you further? Change your tone to a firm command, *"No."* Let it sink in for a few seconds, then immediately resume your soft, wooing sleep song. He didn't quite understand, and tests further? Repeat *"No"* more firmly; wait for his response of recognition, and again resume your loving singing. When he responds to any degree by settling down, let him know of your approval immediately. *"That's right, darling, that's Mother's little son! Now, close your eyes and go to sleep ..."* And resume singing until he falls asleep.

But possibly your child will test still further. If you sense real resistance, then you may give a firm, no-nonsense tap on the leg or bottom. This need not be really painful (though it must be sufficient to bring the desired result). It is simply an attention-getting action, a gentle correction, and in no way punishment! The little one is likely to look at you with astonishment, his feelings hurt, and begin to pucker up. Naturally, this touches your heart, but you may let your instincts govern your response. (Didn't the Good Shepherd comfort the wayward lamb?) Comfort him, and kiss him, for his crying is not rebellion; then continue to tell him to close his eyes and go to sleep, and carry on with intimate conversation and soothing lullabies, until the victory is won. If you will be consistent in following this pattern from the first, exemplifying the spirit you wish to see reflected in your little one, you will open a channel for the Holy Spirit to lead him into a new victory over self—a priceless victory indeed, and a new step in the victorious Christian life—at the age of only a few weeks or months!

What's in a lullaby? —A special time of tenderness and closeness for mother and child, yes, and a most precious opportunity for invoking the true Spirit of the gospel. Jesus once said, *"If ye continue in my word, then are ye my disciples indeed; and ye shall know the truth, and the truth shall make you free ... If the Son therefore shall make you free, ye shall be free indeed"* (John 8:31–36). Just so, the mother makes a sacrifice to prepare the way for her child to continue in *her* word. In so doing she reveals to him the Way, the Truth, and the Life, and he too becomes *"free indeed."*

How fortunate is the child with parents who understand this priceless privilege! He gains an invaluable advantage from this early training, for by habituating this simple kind of obedience, Mother and Father lay the groundwork for a solid conversion. The child's early experience of trust and compliance will give him a natural confidence in his relationship to his heavenly Father as he grows in grace. And these parents have the assurance that their constant prayers for help are heard as they cooperate with the divine agencies in the order of the gospel.

Yours for sweet slumbers—and their rewards ...

"The lessons that we ourselves learn from Christ we should give to our children, as the young minds can receive them, little by little opening to them the beauty of the principles of heaven. Thus the Christian home becomes a school, where the parents serve as underteachers, while Christ Himself is the chief instructor"
(White, *The Desire of Ages*, p. 515.2).

CHAPTER 4:

"Train Up a Child in the Way He Should Go ..."

Dear Young Parents of the Lord's Household,

Many years ago, my husband and I watched an unusual wild animal performance on television, featuring Gunther Gebel-Williams, an animal trainer for nearly forty years. We saw his remarkable act with eighteen beautiful Bengal and Royal Siberian tigers behaving like house pets and going through phenomenal routines. They sat up and begged, two of them played leapfrog, and one hopped on rear paws like a kangaroo. Then four tigers lay down together and rolled over twice. They rubbed against him affectionately, and he cuffed them playfully, and petted them like kittens. Gunther could command all this, as well as directing a herd of thirty-two elephants, by voice alone—no whip cracking or chair waving—a beautiful animal performance!

But what really caught our attention as we read his biography, was the method of his training. The horse trainer who gave him his start taught him that unending patience was the secret of success in training any animal. "Never strike a horse," he explained. "Instead, constantly repeat instructions, using rewards for accomplishments and mild rebukes for failure." Gunther also learned the value of consistency—presenting himself every day to an animal the same way. Friendship has been the key to his training methods. "I am the boss, but they know I am also their friend. I feel very close to my animals."

Finally, he sums up his philosophy like this: "Training is a beautiful thing. To get inside the head of an animal and communicate, that is wonderful. That is what I live for."

What could be a more apt premise for relating to our little children, than to live to get inside their heads and communicate? And the methods Gunther used—consistency, friendship and repetition, natural rewards and mild rebukes—to win the confidence of wild tigers and elephants, are just as appropriate and effective for small, "untamed" people.

Every waking hour in the infant's and child's life is relentlessly providing experiences that cause reactions and responses for good or for bad. The repetition of each experience and response forms patterns of behavior. God has placed in the hands of parents and guardians the opportunity to plan these various experiences, and their constant repetition will naturally establish habits that will form the basis for sound adult decision-making, the ability to govern self and take responsibility—habits that will form strong character. So every detail in the daily routine is weighed carefully with regard to the final outcome of the patterns we establish.

> *Every waking hour in the infant's and child's life is relentlessly providing experiences that cause reactions and responses for good or for bad.*

Let's consider a couple of illustrations. The first scenario might go something like this: It is morning. Little Jared wakes up whenever he feels like it, often crying (which is how children frequently wake up on their own if they have not been regulated). The parents may still be in bed. He is invited to get in with them, and snuggled and comforted until he decides to get down. Soon all the siblings are awake, reacting in their varied ways to the light of day.

When the family demands can no longer be postponed, someone gets up and proceeds to take care of the most clamoring needs.

Then as the family meanders around doing their "thing," gradually working up to breakfast, commands are issued from time to time ... "Hurry up and get dressed" ... "Stop that fussing" ... "Who had that toy first? Give it back right now." Etc., etc. Finally, breakfast is ready, and all are seated at the table in various stages of disarray, and in as many states of ill-temper.

The beds have been left to be made at a more convenient time, clothes are left all over the house, and wet towels and puddles of water decorate the bathroom floor. To add to the confusion, the cat is probably meowing and getting underfoot because her food and water dishes are empty.

The mood for the remainder of the day has been set, and irretrievable opportunities for patterning and positive habit formation have been neglected. But is this all? Sadly, the most unintentional education has taken place. *By default*, these are some of the lessons that have been taught:

1. Insecurity is the norm. The child doesn't know what to expect.

2. Self-indulgence is OK. Getting up happens when one feels like it.

3. The child is in control—not the parent.

4. Crying is OK when you feel a little out of sorts. Sympathy and cuddling imply approval for yielding to natural passion.

5. The responsibilities of life can be postponed and neglected in order to give in to selfish feelings.

6. Obedience is definitely not pleasant.

7. The new day is nothing to get excited about.

You can see that this little one is actually being imprisoned in his babyhood, for his parents have not set him free to look outside of himself and happily to enjoy the responsibilities of self-government. He has also been deprived of the satisfactions of accomplishment. By the continual repetition of these lessons negative habits are formed simply *by default*.

While uncontrolled behavior may be merely an annoyance in babyhood, its continued indulgence ripens and brings to maturity the inevitable fruit. The adult who exhibits this behavior, though in more subtle and socially acceptable forms, becomes a counter-productive member of society. And we know that these patterns are set in the first three years. (White, *Child Guidance*, pp. 194.2, 197.1, 83.1)

Now let's see what a different approach might accomplish. It's 7:00 A.M. Mother and Father are already up and dressed, bed made, and have the household under control. They are free to guide their children calmly through the morning activities. Jennifer is cheerfully and considerately awakened, as she is accustomed to being every morning (until the habit has become well-established). After a stretch or two she climbs out of bed and Mother takes her into her lap for a brief morning snuggle. This affectionate framework provides a perfect setting for a simple wakeup hymn and prayer. Then she is helped into her robe, led into the bathroom, and coached through a carefully planned routine that may be a simple pattern for the rest of her life. Here's one example:

1. Use the toilet.
   a. Use so many squares of tissue (or some safe guide for little ones).
   b. Flush toilet.
   c. Put down cover.
2. Start water in tub (or use shower, depending).
3. Remove pajamas and turn right side out; lay on chair.
4. Get in tub, which is filled to a predetermined line.
5. Beginning with sleepy eyes, proceed efficiently to carefully cleanse rest of body in order, with due respect for every member, instructing, explaining, and demonstrating as suitable.
6. Shampoo hair on specified days.
7. Rinse body, drain tub, and wring out washcloth.
8. Finish with cold splash.
9. Rinse tub for next person.
10. Dry off thoroughly.
11. Put on robe (or wrap with towel).
12. Brush teeth.
13. Hang up washcloth and towel and return to bedroom.
14. Dress (clothes have been laid out the night before, so no time is wasted in decision- making).
15. Hang up pajamas and robe.

CHAPTER 4: "Train Up a Child in the Way He Should Go ..." 43

16. Make bed carefully.

17. Feed and water kitty.

18. Drink water and juice.

19. Quiet free time as reward for dispatch.

20. Breakfast.

We're watching lifelong patterns being formed in an atmosphere of calmness and love, and it is all accomplished without force, using those three simple, primary educational instruments: The Environmental Atmosphere, The Discipline of Habit, and The Presentation of Living Ideas.

What are the lessons taught by this approach?

1. She has the example of her parents to model after.

2. She is subject to home government.

3. There is no time or need for self-pity.

4. Diligence and dispatch have their rewards.

5. Thoroughness brings satisfaction.

6. Purity within and without is fundamental.

7. Consideration is contagious and gives joy to all.

8. That the new day may be met with glad anticipation.

In learning the joy of self-government, she is set free from perpetual babyhood, and receives the natural rewards of accomplishment.

"But," you might say, "this is absolutely too structured. There is no variety. Where is the freedom to break away for creative enterprises? Doesn't this produce stilted, mechanical personalities?"

Here is a practical illustration that took place this morning. My husband received a call last week from a young woman requesting a piano tuning. She said, "Mr. Shafer, you were recommended to us by the piano store. We have a lot of confidence in them and they say you're 'the best,' that you keep your appointments and are fair and honest. We would like you to take over the care of our piano on a permanent basis and keep it in good order." An appointment was made.

At the appointed hour Mr. Shafer was met at the gate by the mother (a former teacher) and two little children, five and three, all cheerfully anticipating his visit.

"How do you do? I'm Gordon Shafer."

"How do you do, Mr. Shafer? (smiling). I'm Karen. And this is Michael."

"Hello, Mr. Shafer (smiling)."

"And this is Laura."

"Hello, Mr. Shafer (smiling)."

They all proceeded in a very natural and comfortable way to help him carry his tools into the cheerful and inviting home and show him where the piano was. Then during the next couple of hours while the piano was being tuned, they carried out pre-planned activities. For twenty minutes or so they drew. For another period of time they engaged in some other quiet activity. Then they all put on warm clothes and went out in the weather to rake leaves from the patio. Everyone knew what to do; the mother, with the children, was accomplishing her activities on schedule; the children knew just what to expect and were happily carrying it out. Conflicts were absent and unnecessary.

There was no self-consciousness upon meeting a stranger. They didn't ignore him or fidget uncomfortably or run up teasingly, saying, "I'll bite you, I'll bite you," because they didn't know what to say. They naturally and comfortably participated in the accepted conventionalities because their mother had taught them, not only by her own example, but also by patterning and structure. She had shown them what to expect and how to meet it.

They naturally and comfortably participated in the accepted conventionalities because their mother had taught them, not only by her own example, but also by patterning and structure. She had shown them what to expect and how to meet it.

They were self-possessed and nice to be around because they had been programmed to behave acceptably. It was second nature.

CHAPTER 4: "Train Up a Child in the Way He Should Go ..."   45

This seeming miracle was not accomplished by making exceptions to the rules (exceptions and variations may come later, after the habits are well established), but by careful planning and strict organization. This mother was even particular to choose a piano tuner that kept his appointments on time, so that her schedule could be structured to include it.

The higher the desired goal, the more critical is the organization necessary to achieve that goal. The Emergency Room Trauma Center at Children's Hospital in Washington, D.C. functions as a prime example of a system that serves as a model of lifesaving techniques, essentially because of closely integrated pre-planning and teamwork. It is also heartening because it shows how organization is not only useful in establishing a successful endeavor, but in correcting a disastrous situation as well. Here's how this remarkable transformation was described by the reporters:

> The physician in charge, Dr. Eichelberger, turned a code blue from a scene where 15–25 medical personnel converged in a spectacle more like a football scrimmage than a medical consultation, into a smoothly coordinated team operating at full capacity to save lives ... Dr. Eichelberger first set up two trauma bays available 24 hours a day for admission and resuscitation of victims. The two bays were stocked with all the tools and supplies necessary to treat serious trauma injuries and medical emergencies. A special team was designated and given its own code. They devised a checklist and divided it among team members so that everyone had a role and the checklist got completed faster. The people who didn't have to be inside the code room—such as the X-ray and lab technicians—were designated the 'outer core,' and they stood outside, instantly available. The 'inner core' consisted of just those nurses and doctors necessary to work the checklist. The results were impressive. Critically injured children survived more than 97% of the time. There was no magic about it.
>
> Dr. Eichelberger made no new medical discoveries. He simply began to apply state-of-the-art medicine in a "methodical manner."

Don't we have access through the gospel to "state-of-the-art" educational principles?

And can't we, too, expect impressive results by applying them in a "methodical manner"?

God Himself personifies system and order. Our very existence depends upon split-second timing and integrated action. Everything happens according to a carefully planned schedule. "God's purposes know no haste and no delay" (White, *The Desire of Ages*, p. 321.1). And as His children we will function with Him and bring our households into a natural and happy order that will be a positive influence in society wherever it may exist. "The Lord has shown that gospel order has been too much feared and neglected ... Formality should be shunned; but, in so doing, order should not be neglected. There is order in heaven. There was order in the church when Christ was upon the earth, and after His departure order was strictly observed among His apostles. And now in these last days, while God is bringing his children into the unity of the faith, there is more real need of order than ever before" (White, *Early Writings*, p. 97.1).

"I saw that everything in heaven was in perfect order. Said the angel, 'Look ye, Christ is the head, move in order, move in order. Have a meaning to everything. Said the angel, behold how perfect, how beautiful the order in heaven. Follow it" (White, Ms.11, 12/25/1850).

As we enter into His plan, our success is assured.

Yours for the joys of loving organization ...

"In dealing with your children, follow the method of the gardener. By gentle touches, by loving ministrations, seek to fashion their characters after the pattern of the character of Christ" (White, *Child Guidance,* p. 36.3).

CHAPTER 5:
Of Little Acorns and Mighty Oaks

Dear Young Parents of the Lord's Household,

One spring, while reading directions for planting seeds indoors for an early garden, I noticed this bit of advice: "When planting seeds in flats, a lean soil is best. No need to begin feeding until the true leaves are formed and plants are ready for transplant." And here I was, thinking that I'd give them an extra boost by placing them in rich soil—and even adding plant food!

But the seed contains in itself sufficient life and the proper amount of nutrients to support its early development at a safe and normal rate.

So I followed directions. I chose an environment that would be conducive to growth—light and moisture carefully regulated. The seeds were properly spaced and covered. And then I waited. For long days I watched over the seedbed, never relaxing my vigilance. The development took place quietly, imperceptibly. I simply took the responsibility of faithful watchfulness, supplying the necessary elements at the appropriate time, and controlling the environment, protecting from heat and cold, drought and blast, and destructive pests. And one day I was rewarded with a beautiful crop of healthy seedlings.

Our interest in growing an outstanding "home garden" prompts a striking analogy. Is it possible that as parents and educators we might be overfeeding at a critical time in the development of the small persons in our care? Are we neglecting to allow time and opportunity for the inherent reserves to quietly germinate and unfold? And yes, just how *do* little acorns develop into strong and mighty oaks? Is it accomplished by force-feeding and exposure to all the elements?

Let's take a closer look at the nature of the germination and early growth of infancy and childhood, the so-called formative years—years that shape all future growth. We know that over-stimulation in any of the primary areas—physical, mental, moral, or spiritual—will unbalance the system and result in disproportionate development. Any deformity that takes place here may never be fully corrected. But at the same time, prudent nurturing during this period produces vigorous stock from which optimum growth can proceed.

Think of the wonderful processes taking place in the first few years of childhood, the motor skills—reaching, grasping, crawling, walking, and running; the development of sight and hearing, smelling, feeling, and tasting; the social skills in inter-family relationships; and the spiritual perceptions of love and sympathy. It is only as these things are developed harmoniously that information can be assimilated. If information is forced upon the developing mind prematurely, it is not prepared to receive it. The pathways become jammed, and natural inquisitiveness is stifled. Indeed, crowding the mind with material that cannot be put to practical use is establishing a propensity for forgetfulness, and the memory becomes impaired. And so the hope of lovely, mature fruit is disappointed through forcing a precocious ripening.

The plan that the Creator instigated in Eden so long ago must still be the paradigm for the Christian home today. We see an explosion of scientific discovery and technology. Social mores are turned upside-down; but in this changing environment there is still no suitable replacement for the family structure as the perfect nurturing environment for its offspring.

The simple setting of the Christian home provides all the facilities and motivation necessary for the education of its children for the first few years. Little financial outlay is necessary for educational aids, for the child needs no special "child environment." The home itself offers a complete curriculum with facilities perfectly adapted to its purpose.

Consider how physical, moral, and social development takes place in the family. Who hasn't marveled at the way a six-month-old watches with dawning understanding as she sees a spoonful of food travel from dish to Mother's mouth, and hungrily reaches for the spoon herself? Or watched a toddler as he sees Father squeeze out the toothpaste on the toothbrush and put it in his mouth? Just hand him his own little brush and watch

CHAPTER 5: Of Little Acorns and Mighty Oaks

> *The simple setting of the Christian home provides all the facilities and motivation necessary for the education of its children for the first few years.*

how perfectly he mimics every motion. At the appropriate time, all that is necessary to teach the little one to ask a blessing before meals is perhaps to help him fold his hands, and he does just what he has been watching his models doing for some time, squinting his eyes shut, and without prompting, even lisping his baby form of grace as Mother prays.

And the social skills—how much depends on the interrelationships at home with Mother and Father and siblings in the first few years. Then the extended family and guests gradually expand opportunities for interaction—all without pressure from peers, or competition.

Imagine the imperceptible growth taking place beneath the surface before there is any sign of response. You'll find this pattern recurring periodically. Just as it takes nine months for the development of the fetus in the womb before it is revealed as a fully formed little individual, so each new stage of growth is preceded by a time of concealed development that calls for patient waiting on the part of those wise parents who allow time and freedom for this delicate process to occur.

No force is ever involved in this setting, for we are reminded of that primary premise for true education, which is, "Forced education is false education." A natural motivation is always present. There is no need for artificial incentives, rewards, rivalry, or diplomas, to accomplish the desired results. Love is all. The majority of teaching is done by example. Jesus confirmed this divine principle when He said, *"The Son can do nothing of himself, but what He seeth the Father do: for what things soever he doeth, these also doeth the Son likewise. For the Father loveth the Son, and sheweth him all things that himself doeth ..."* (John 5:19, 20).

Modesty, truthfulness, purity, kindness, courtesy, obedience, carefulness, thoroughness, are all learned at the mother's side by imitation and gentle instruction. These basic attributes should be acquired before the social horizons widen beyond the home. We have a special testimony from the Lord to guide us in applying these lessons:

> A child's first school should be his home. His first instructors should be his father and his mother. His first lessons should be

lessons of respect, obedience, reverence, and self-control... In the home-school our boys and girls are being prepared to attend a church-school when they reach a proper age to associate more intimately with other children (White, *Manuscript Releases*, vol. 8, pp. 4.3–5.1).

So we see that children are not ready to associate closely with other children until these lessons have been learned. With these habits well established they are secure in their new relationships because they know how to act. Because they have become habituated in right doing, they are prepared to take a stand for the right instead of weakly yielding to the popular majority. They are able to take leadership, with befitting maturity.

Modesty, truthfulness, purity, kindness, courtesy, obedience, carefulness, thoroughness, are all learned at the mother's side by imitation and gentle instruction.

Picture a roomful of wigglers, periodically uprooted from their natural environment in order to receive a conventional religious education. What teacher can hope to elicit a free spiritual response while trying to keep order and engage the attention of this group of excited children who are much more interested in interacting with each other? And what true mother would willingly deprive herself and her child of the sweet spiritual privileges that are theirs by divine mandate? If little ones are taken into situations where they are compelled to interact with their peers before they have become established in these primary lessons, they receive their education from their equals—and their education will rise no higher than its source. And it's easy to see that it takes several years to establish this readiness.

> During the first six or seven years of a child's life, special attention should be given to its physical training, rather than the intellect ... Parents, especially mothers, should be the only teachers of such infant minds. They should not educate from books. The children will generally be inquisitive to learn the things of nature.... The mother's loving instruction at a tender age is what is needed by children in the formation of character (White, *Child Guidance,* p. 300.3, 4).

Yet current practice introduces educational experiences outside of the home at a very early age, "the sooner the better." Instead of "the parents, especially the mother," being "the only teachers" of these infant minds, they are relinquishing their wonderful privileges and duties. Instead of carefully preparing these little ones in the home school through symmetrical preparation for advanced learning experiences, parents are urged to introduce peer learning experiences, and to encourage the reading of many books. Educators emphasize the importance of exposing children to books even in infancy, stressing the value of encouraging an early love for reading. When the child begins kindergarten and grade school, prizes are offered to those who read the most books. It is assumed that this will pattern a reading habit that will provide a flow of information, ensuring the growth of intelligence.

However, there is another side to the coin that many early educators considered of far greater consequence in the development of the child's intellect. They knew that the child's development was multi-faceted. The early years of growth encompassed much more than intellectual advancement. Physical health was indispensable—actually prerequisite—to mental development. The spiritual nature completed the triumvirate, the proportionate development of all three being the desired goal.

We hear much even today about the wholeness of the human system and the close relationship of mind and body. But unfortunately, much has been lost in the understanding of God's plan in the perfection of body, soul, and spirit, and in applying His eternal principles in the education of our little ones. "True education" is a growing up into Christ, a strong and symmetrical plant in the Lord's vineyard.

What about books, then? Shouldn't we at least provide nature books to help them understand the natural world around them? Herbert Spencer once said, "Reading is seeing by proxy." How much superior is the very real knowledge gained through intimate acquaintance with a live puppy than in reading about one in a book, seeing a picture, or in handling a stuffed model; or how much closer the bond with the Creator Himself is a walk through the fields gathering wild flowers, than sitting indoors with a flower picture book.

Anne Sullivan Macy, that remarkable teacher who liberated the mind of a child who could neither see, hear, nor speak, shows great insight in her approach: "I am beginning to suspect," she said, "all elaborate systems of education. They seem to me to be built up on the supposition that every child is a kind of idiot who must be taught to think. Whereas, if the child is left to himself, he will think more and better, if less showily. Let him go and come freely. Let him touch real things and combine his impressions for himself, instead of sitting indoors at a little round table, while a sweet-voiced teacher suggests that he build a stone wall with his wooden blocks, or make a rainbow out of colored strips of paper, or plant straw trees in bead flower pots. Such teaching fills the mind with artificial associations that must be got rid of, before the child can develop independent ideas out of actual experience."[4]

Even for older students, Ellen White wrote, "Instead of confining their study to that which men have said or written, let students be directed to the sources of truth, to the vast fields opened for research in nature and revelation. Let them contemplate the great facts of duty and destiny, and the mind will expand and strengthen" (*Education*, p. 17.2).

You will notice that we are talking here about good books—not trashy novels or fantasy or even nonsense. Arthur Spalding, a well-respected SDA educator, taught that "An all-round education demands interests which lead to physical work and to creative mental activity. Good books have their value, but they are a poor substitute for the broader education every child should receive. Our children are being overloaded with studies and reading. The relief must come, not by bare deprivation, but by substitution of a comprehensive and rational education."

Supposing, now, that this natural plan has been followed—this *"comprehensive and rational education,"* and the child has formed a strong physical constitution. The lessons from nature—in its largest sense—have laid a foundation of broad experience. The time has now come to extend the educational dimensions upward by opening before this ready little mind the Word of God. Thus far the parents, in their constant interaction, have been the primary channels of spiritual enlightenment. Now the dawning intelligence, supported by a robust constitution, is ready first to hear, and then to read first hand, that sacred history, poetry, prophecy, doctrine, that will be the foundation for all future education. The perceptive mother will recognize readiness, and she will discover that motivation has naturally taken place.

Before any other books are introduced, it will be to his everlasting advantage if the child is first securely bonded to the Holy Scriptures. Let him be nurtured and thrilled with the wonderful stories, in their proper order, just as they are presented in Holy Writ, without being distracted in any way by other reading matter. Yes, even in the beautiful and classic English of the King James Version, if you desire, for it will be just as easily

---

[4] By Anne Sullivan Macy in Helen Keller's autobiography, *The Story of My Life*, p. 319.

learned at this age as his mother tongue, and it's a marvelous way to form the taste to the highest ideals in literature. Illustrations? The uninhibited child imagination will create pristine mental images superior by far to any artists' portrayals.

"Do not think that the Bible will become a tiresome book to the children. Under a wise instructor the word will become more and more desirable. It will be to them as the bread of life. It will never grow old. There is in it a freshness and a beauty that attract and charm the children and youth" (White, *Counsels to Parents, Students, and Teachers,* p. 171.3).

The first lessons from the Scriptures may take place each day at a specially arranged time. Choose a quiet place where there will be no interruptions, and you can be close to your child. Then begin systematically to read in sequence the stories of the Old Testament. You remember that the child Jesus' early education consisted of these very scriptures, as did every true Jewish child. Read them just as they are written, only omitting things like too lengthy passages. Let the child's readiness be your guide. And don't be afraid of repetition—it will naturally lead to the joys of memorization.

While some unusual words may require explanation, try to resist the tendency to define every unfamiliar word. Robert Southey, a writer well-respected for his observations, once commented perceptively, "What blockheads are those wise persons, who think it necessary that a child should comprehend everything it reads" (From the book, *The Doctor, &c.* (1872), p. 87.). This is so true, as you've probably already observed. Children listening to unfamiliar words in sentence and paragraph settings will find most definitions to be self-evident. And isn't that the way we learn language at the outset, just by listening to strange sounds and associating them with known activities and objects and sensations? The very process of thinking them out develops creativity, stimulates the imagination, and gives valuable exercise to the mental powers. It's important to allow perfect freedom for this personal development. Remember the seeds germinating below the surface? Prompting and testing are destructive to this delicate process.

In comparison to this divine plan, what can common children's literature contribute? Vocabulary is meager; ideas and format are simplistic. Subject matter is largely nonsense. And by its very nature it is all reduced to what is thought to be a "child's level," which necessarily inhibits normal maturation. Fantasy is used to stimulate the imagination and spirit the child away to another world. The mind is excited and led into imaginary situations that must sooner or later be abandoned, for they are not part of the human experience. At some point in time the one who has found a kind of fulfillment in illusion will be disillusioned. Valuable resources—precious time, nervous energy, and most crucial of all, trust—are lost in the process.

Not so with Bible truth. It is continually being put to practical use and will never be irrelevant. The structure whose building blocks are Truth needs not to be periodically torn apart to have faulty or obsolete materials replaced. These building blocks have already been tested and tried and remain as solid support forever.

Classic children's literature capitalizes on the theme of contest between good and evil, depicted in various characters and plots. But Christian parents have in hand sacred history that demonstrates the conflict in reality, with true heroes and the ultimate triumph of right over wrong. Rather than exploiting childish credulity by creating imaginary contests between counterfeit villains and saviors, it is the parents' obligation to lead them to understand the real controversy of the ages, preparing them to meet the real foe.

Instead of fastening their attention on make-believe creatures, we may lead them to the One who loves little children and is able to keep from every evil, day and night. "The Lord is my Shepherd" (Psalm 23:1.), and "He shall cover thee with His feathers," (Psalm 91:4), will be ideas to capture their imaginations. Their trust may be freely placed in the real protecting presence of faithful guardian angels. These favored children will not be frightened by nightmares of "monsters," but will easily be comforted with the truth, as the Holy Spirit enters in to aid the parents in their endeavors. The confidence that these young ones have placed in us will deepen as the years go by, for they know we can always be counted on to give them truth.

And now, what about that love of knowledge that we want to instill in our children? We have postponed introducing them to books. We have confined their first literary experience to the Bible. Isn't it possible they will thereby be disadvantaged throughout all their future education? Johann Spurzheim (1776–1832), a well-known early authority on the physiology and function of the human brain, made this interesting observation: "Experience demonstrates that of any number of children of equal intellectual powers, those who receive no particular care in infancy, and who do not begin to study till the constitution begins to be consolidated, but who enjoy the benefit of a good physical education, very soon surpass in their studies those who commenced earlier, and who read numerous books when very young."⁵ This is confirmed by Samuel Auguste Tissot (1728–1797), an early Swiss physician, who adds, "Of ten infants, destined for different vocations, I should prefer that the one who is to study through life should be the least learned at the age of twelve."⁶

But beyond all this, by carrying out these divine principles, we have prepared the way for the Holy Spirit to gain access to the heart. These learners may have more understanding than their teachers, for the Lord's testimonies are their meditation (Psalm 119:99). We have taken the principal steps in setting their spirits free. And the promise is, *"And all thy children shall be taught by the LORD"* (Isaiah 54:13, NIV). David tells us, *"And he shall be like a tree planted by the rivers of water, that bringeth forth his fruit in his season; his leaf also shall not wither; and whatsoever he doeth shall prosper"* (Psalm 1:3).

Yours for nurturing sturdy seedlings ...

A Sower Went Forth...

Happy Mother's Day to Mine;
For mine's the best, you know.
I bear her stamp in my design;
The things she thought important, show.

But not for show she bent the twig;
Her love was so devoid of pride...
The cause she sought was really big;
She wanted Truth to be my guide.

So on and on through life I go,
Still chanting, "Show me Truth!"
And all the gems I find just grow
From seeds she planted in my youth.

—Geoffrey

---

5 *Dictionary of Thoughts*, Standard Publishing Co. (1965), p. 166.
6 Ibid.

Then, What About Punishment?

The following representative examples, and how they were met with understanding and purpose, involved a three-and-a-half-year-old, who had not been trained and habituated to obedience and cooperation, yet was still impressionable, and responsive to right principles and genuine, loving attention.

It would surely be a rare child who never needed to be corrected. After all, we have sinful natures to contend with. But if we will put the divine elements to practical use, upon which *Letters to Parents* chapters one through five are founded, we find that correction is usually of a mild nature. For the rare instance when firm, disinterested punishment may be necessary, a single experience, when given in a true spirit, may often be all that is necessary to touch a tender heart and restore trust and submission. Right habits, built upon a strong relationship of love, will work to great advantage, for they place us, as well as our children, on God's side in life's battles.

The following practical demonstrations, taken from real life, are examples of methods that support these divine principles. Substantial victories are obtained, because they *disarm* anger and rebellion through *the conquests of divine love,* instead of engaging in destructive conflict. The foundation is reinforced in the process, which will support established patterns of behavior in a productive relationship, and mutual respect is strengthened without crushing the tender will of a little child.

The influence of love leads to harmony and happiness, rather than to the bitterness and distrust which must follow the use of force and angry punishment.

The influence of love leads to harmony and happiness, rather than to the bitterness and distrust which must follow the use of force and angry punishment. It establishes a proper respect of authority, without destroying the power of self-government. And what an advantage it is to retain the precious relationships that have been developed through the careful groundwork that has been laid over time, through wise and judicious parental management!

Perhaps these four examples will stimulate creative thoughts in your mind and heart, as the Holy Spirit lends His impress, enabling you to find solutions to unique issues that may arise in *your* experience.

CHARACTER BY DESIGN
PRACTICAL APPLICATIONS

EXERCISE #1

PROBLEM:

Display of passion in sacred services.

OBJECTIVE:

To maintain the educational environment; to disarm the wrong spirit.

ILLUSTRATION:

Jesse, a dear little strong-willed, unprepared three-and-a-half-year-old, is angry and lashing out at Mother during her testimony, revealing a defiant spirit in his dark looks and demands for attention.

PREVENTIVE/CORRECTIVE:

Without a knowledge of what preceded this display we won't deal with the preventive now, except to say that as a rule this kind of issue can be forestalled with prudent preparation.

The corrective was handled this way: Grandmother stepped to Jesse's side, took him in her lap with a smile, held him firmly but gently, letting him know by this action that things were in control, and that he was not compelled to continue his agitation. He found in loving arms security and protection from a wrong spirit.

LESSONS LEARNED IN THIS EXPERIMENT:

1. *THE CHILD FINDS REST IN LOVING AUTHORITY.* He finds a sense of peace in this unexpected development. This welcome diversion reveals a ray of hope, akin to the sinner's relief when Jesus brings that "Blessed Assurance."

2. *THAT MOTHER HAS SUPPORT.* Even though Mother was not able to deal with his problem at the moment, there was unity on the part of all the adults in the child's world, and he could not take advantage of her preoccupation.

3. *THE SPIRIT OF LOVE SET HIM FREE.* Love and firmness disarmed the defiant spirit and resolved the conflict in his breast. There was no competition, thus no more conflict.

4. *REVERENCE.* No interference with the order of the sacred service is going to be permitted.

EXERCISE #2

PROBLEM:

Delay tactics when called.

OBJECTIVE:

To program prompt and eager response.

ILLUSTRATION:

Jesse is called to lunch. He ignores the call, makes up excuses, or tries to divert Mother's attention to something else; or he may declare that he is not coming until he goes to the bathroom.

PREVENTIVE/CORRECTIVE:

When it's time for dinner, Mother goes to Jesse and takes a brief but genuine interest in his activity. Then she comments that dinner is almost ready. "Let's put this away so that we'll be ready to go wash up as soon as the first bell rings." Get big sister's cooperation to ring the bell at the proper time. Then cheerfully lead him into the bathroom, showing him method in washing up and combing his hair. Be his companion and friend in this process; the two of you are working together to meet the appointment. Make it pleasant and instructive.

A story giving an account of how prompt obedience saved a life, or how delay brought disappointment or disaster, will be very useful at an early opportunity. A well-chosen Bible story or real-life story will be fine. As you draw a simple parallel, without belaboring the point, showing how it is important to come at once when Mother calls, he'll quickly make the connection.

NEVER call him without leading him into the response, until you have certain evidence that he is habituated to the process and will not fail. Every success, whether led by the mother or on his own, will breed success; every failure will breed failure.

Practice, practice, practice—consistently, together—until the habit of cooperation is formed.

LESSONS LEARNED IN THIS EXPERIMENT:

1. Mother is a reliable mentor. SHE DEMONSTRATES what is expected of him.

2. There is NO OPPORTUNITY TO DELAY or avoid the command.

3. There is NO PLACE FOR COMPETITION.

4. He is not at liberty to order his own life. He is a HAPPY SUBJECT of higher authority.

5. LOVE IS THE POWER of the law.

6. He has gained A NEW MEASURE OF SELF-CONTROL without resistance on his part, by not allowing a need for punishment to develop.

EXERCISE #3

PROBLEM:

Cruelty to God's creatures.

OBJECTIVE:

To structure responsibility and kindness in this small realm, in order to lay a foundation for applying these principles in larger relationships as he advances in understanding and grows in grace.

ILLUSTRATION:

Tomato Worms: Handled injudiciously, starved; taken out of natural environment which is not replaced with a suitable substitute; inconsistent care and feeding; suffering and death of worms.

He assumes that he can have the pleasures of nature without taking responsibility for obeying nature's laws (which, by the way, are included with God's moral law). Think of the implications when this attitude is allowed to continue on into the moral obligations of later life.

Negative lessons are impressed upon his mind and heart in this unguided setting that hinder the development of benevolence and true love. They will have to be unlearned before he can truly understand love, obedience, and sincerity.

PREVENTIVE/CORRECTIVE:

Mother takes advantage of this interest by using it as an educational tool. Here is a natural motivation, something that he has a strong interest in. Mother shows her interest and goes with Jesse to find worms, calling attention to their food and environment, and planning with him how to protect the worm's welfare in a captive environment.

Together they find a jar, make holes in the lid, fill it to a proper depth with soil for the development of the chrysalis, place fresh leaves and a stem to crawl on. They take the worm and examine it, noticing the markings, color, "horn," etc. Mother lets Jesse turn it over and look at it to his heart's content, all the while instructing him to be gentle and thoughtful of the worm's feelings. (Worms do have feelings as Jesse knows, for he doesn't even like to leave them alone for fear they will be lonely!) So, build on his natural compassion, and extend it as far as he can understand.

After a suitable length of time suggest that the worm is looking for his food and would be happy if he were put where he can eat and do what he needs to do.

Designate a safe place to keep the jar where it can be easily observed, and allow it to be taken down only at specially planned times, to feed and observe, and hold for brief periods. Mother must plan these feeding times in her schedule consistently until project is complete. Story time each day is used to educate in the life cycle of the tomato worm, and as it goes through its cycle a genuine interest is shown by Mother and family.

Then, since tomato worms destroy our food supply, Jesse may be taught a proper way to eliminate as many as he can find—except the ones he is watching and caring for. This can be done in a compassionate spirit, using the least painful and easiest way to perform a necessary task. Our responsibility to protect the natural environment always involves hard choices. This is a lesson that children will naturally understand and accept if allowed to serve in the spirit of true sacrifice. The effects of sin and death in this world are evident to even the youngest children, and this natural experience affords a wonderful opportunity to open their minds to the plan of creation. These creatures were not destructive in the garden of Eden, but the entrance of sin changed the nature of all of God's creation, even in the animal kingdom.

Jesse can be told how God gave man dominion over all His creatures, and that means that he is to love and care for them, preserve balance, and keep them from destroying the earth. Then the concept of the perfection of the earth made new, with no pests to destroy, can be developed from time to time, as you have opportunities together.

He won't be encouraged to keep many of them. He'll find that they develop into moths that will produce many more enemies to our garden, and then would only have to be destroyed. (Help him to arrive at this conclusion himself, if possible.) So Mother assists him in keeping his "worm farm" manageable—just big enough to learn their life cycle and satisfy his interest.

LESSONS LEARNED IN THIS EXPERIMENT:

1. CAREFULNESS, GENTLENESS,

2. KINDNESS to the living creatures within his environment. As he develops this quality in this childish relationship, it will, with consistent attention, be applied ever more broadly with developing maturity, to the expanding relationships with all who are in need of tenderness, compassion, and sensitivity.

3. RESPONSIBILITY. With Mother's companionship and interest, Jesse is educated and habituated to care regularly and thoughtfully for these pets.

4. PATIENCE. As he must wait patiently for the appropriate times to handle the caterpillars, he also learns to wait patiently for them to hatch from the chrysalis.

5. SELF-SACRIFICE. His own interests are set aside in order to carry this responsibility, but because he is motivated, it is not resented.

6. FULFILLMENT. As he is helped to carry this project to a successful conclusion, he gains a sense of satisfaction in a job well done—an invaluable preparation for the next step.

7. A BEFITTING FEAR OF MOTHER. That Mother is wiser than he is, and is responsible to a higher law. Therefore, this is a critical foundation and preparation for:

8. OBEDIENCE.

9. A HEALTHIER RESPECT FOR AUTHORITY. He does things just as Mother instructs, not as he thinks best or desires. But it is all so pleasant that this is not seen as a restriction.

10. A deeper, truer LOVE for his worms, and this adds a new dimension to his love for all. The JOY of service and self-denial.

EXERCISE #4

PROBLEM:

Table manners.

OBJECTIVE:

To structure acceptable eating habits. To help the child understand true thoughtfulness and consideration for others, and that the privilege of eating with others at the family table is earned, and is dependent upon the acquisition of appropriate behavior and gracious manners.

ILLUSTRATION:

Eating at table with fingers, or licking fingers, playing with food, chewing with mouth open, dillydallying, being messy with butter, elbows on table, general messiness, not finishing when others are through, etc.

PREVENTIVE/CORRECTIVE:

Many families allow their children to come to the family table long before they are able to conform to the family standards of mealtime behavior. Consequently, the child has nothing to strive for. Like any other adult privilege, there should be a preparation and demonstration of ability before the privilege is conferred. If this isn't done, naturally it is assumed by the child that his behavior is acceptable.

The alternative is either to make mealtime a time of nagging and unpleasantness in trying to make a proper child out of an unmotivated little animal, or to ignore his behavior, thereby tacitly giving him unearned approval.

The solution is to prepare a suitable learning environment and structure these prerequisites prior to inviting the child to the common table. He will need to have a loving instructor, and much help and encouragement.

There are any number of ways to accomplish this, but here is one way: Mother sets up a table for Jesse before the rest of the family eats. She is there beside him to LEAD him through the meal. She prepares his food simply (before he sits down, as much as possible), so that he does not have to tackle things beyond his capabilities. For instance, she cuts up his salad in bite sizes; butters his bread in small pieces; scoops out his baked potato and prepares it. She makes it as easy as possible for him to eat neatly.

As he is eating, she is there beside him to converse about their common interests, and is ready to assist and instruct in any way that is needed. When he is through—and he must be regulated as to how long it is to take—he may be washed up and either put down for a nap or given some quiet activity in proximity to the family meal.

His readiness to enter in with the family may be tested from time to time when it is certain that he will not be challenged beyond his learned abilities. He may perhaps be allowed to participate on Sabbaths, or when Father comes home. He should be helped to feel it is a happy privilege, and that he is demonstrating his maturity. Of course, it goes without saying that we are all setting an example that he can safely follow.

"The religion of Christ never degrades the receiver; it never makes him coarse or rough, discourteous or self-important ..." (White, *Testimonies for the Church,* vol. 8, p. 63.3).

"Be polite to God and to one another. Remember that He wants you to have the best of manners, that you may glorify Him before the world" (White, *Sons and Daughters of God*, p. 315.5).

LESSONS LEARNED IN THIS EXPERIMENT:

1. THERE ARE RULES, and that THEY ARE OBEYED. (Rules are not changed should they be broken.)

2. THE CHILD IS UNDER AUTHORITY. He sees that his privileges are dependent upon his submission to the rules.

3. Goals may be achieved through COOPERATION with Mother and EFFORT on his part.

4. There are NATURAL REWARDS FOR ACHIEVEMENT.

5. The pleasure of SELF-CONTROL and THOUGHTFULNESS FOR OTHERS.

6. SUBMISSION TO AUTHORITY, without punishment.

7. THE HEALTHY FEAR OF MOTHER, later to be translated into Godly fear.

(cont.)

8. Another lesson in the relationship of teacher to disciple, and THE JOYS OF WORKING TOGETHER.

9. That COOPERATION LEADS TO LIBERTY.

10. COMPLIANCE may be achieved WITHOUT COMPETITION.

Summary

"*Habits, often repeated, make character.* Children who allow themselves to speak rudely to one another, and to be impolite at home, are forming habits that will cling to them in after life, and that will be most difficult to overcome. They do not show that they fear the Lord. They do not manifest refinement of character; their disposition becomes coarse, lacking in civility and that which constitutes *refinement of manners;* and all this casts a reflection upon the home training. In the behavior of children away from home, strangers can read, as in an open book, the history of the home life. They read there of duties left undone, of want of thoughtfulness, of lack of self-forgetfulness, of a disposition toward strife, fretfulness, impatience; while those who show that they have the fear of the Lord before them will, in character and in words, testify of a home where love is cherished, where there is peace, where patience is cultivated, where attention is given to *the little proprieties of life,* each mindful of his duty to make others happy...

"Are you all preparing to become members of the heavenly family? Are you seeking in the home life to be fitted to become members of the Lord's family? If so, make the home life happy by mutual self-sacrifice. If we want Jesus in our home, let kind words be spoken there. *The angels of God will not abide in a home where there is strife and contention.* Let love be cherished, and peace *and Christian politeness,* and angels will be your guests.

"If children and youth seek to be kind and courteous at home, thoughtfulness will become an abiding habit. *Every-day politeness will cause them to be always polite. HOME IS THE VERY PLACE IN WHICH TO PRACTICE* self-denial and thoughtfulness to each member of the family; thus it is with the family in heaven, thus it will be when the scattered families of earth are reunited in the heavenly home."

—Ellen G. White, *Sons and Daughters of God,* p. 113.2–4, emphasis added.

* * *

These principles should help us to hold the standard high at all times. It's a temptation to "let down" at home, with "only the family" around, but it is here that our faithfulness is proved. If noble ideals are not consistently maintained in the family circle, things inevitably deteriorate, and instead of advancing in Christian grace and refinement, the family becomes increasingly degraded. This is where we may practice self-sacrifice at its most basic level, for it is those closest to us that deserve *our best manners, our best appearance, and our deepest love;* and our home becomes in reality, "a little bit of heaven on earth."

TEACH Services, Inc.
PUBLISHING

We invite you to view the complete
selection of titles we publish at:
www.TEACHServices.com

We encourage you to write us
with your thoughts about this,
or any other book we publish at:
info@TEACHServices.com

TEACH Services' titles may be purchased in
bulk quantities for educational, fund-raising,
business, or promotional use.
bulksales@TEACHServices.com

Finally, if you are interested in seeing
your own book in print, please contact us at:
publishing@TEACHServices.com
We are happy to review your manuscript at no charge.

www.ingramcontent.com/pod-product-compliance
Lightning Source LLC
Chambersburg PA
CBHW042133160426
43199CB00021B/2904